The One Girl Gremlin

Phoebe Stuckes

VERVE
POETRY PRESS
BIRMINGHAM

PUBLISHED BY VERVE POETRY PRESS
https://vervepoetrypress.com
mail@vervepoetrypress.com

FIRST PUBLISHED SEP 2021

Printed and bound in the UK
by Positive Print, Birmingham

ISBN: 978-1-912565-64-1

CONTENTS

1. I wake up early, I wait for the light to roll in   9

2. Paris   10

3. Holes   11

4. Dustbunny   12

5. Foxes   13

6 Men's Rooms   14

7. I love you so much   15

8. Free Anna Delvey   16

9. I used to be thin   17

10. Last night I dreamt I was alive and   18

11. Sex Scene   19

12. The one girl gremlin   20

13. Cyberspace   21

14. Dolly Parton   22

15. Baby you know what I want   23

16. Jane Fonda   24

17. Crows   25

18. Pastoral   26

19. Killbuck   27

20. Poem in which I am always leaving   28

21. It's a bad business   29

Acknowledgements

The One Girl Gremlin

I wake up early, I wait for the light to roll in

One minute everything in the world is a poem,
the next everything is a cardboard box
with a number drawn on. I spend my mornings
trying not to imagine all the terrible things
that are happening in the world, somewhere they are
all happening at once. All the rich men with their various wants
their desires lying around like oil stains on the chaise.

Paris

All I think about is love and money, marrying for money and falling
in love on the side. Staying in love with my past loves, meeting them
in oyster bars, never forgetting anything, never making any money.
I think about Jean Rhys in Paris, waiting for Harrison Ford
to wire her some money, she was always dying her hair, getting fired,
falling short on love and money. Did I say Harrison Ford?
I meant Ford Maddox Ford, he had so much money. When I watched
Parade's End I thought I could be the little suffragette who loved him,
as if I could stand a passionless existence shut away in a girls school,
earning my little money. He never tells her how he is feeling.
I don't want that kind of love or money. I want to be stinking drunk
in a restaurant eating bread from a basket, thinking of vintage Prada
and snow. I'll take the love or the money.

Holes

The truth feels repetitive like if you were to fall down a hole in the street and hurt yourself, once, perhaps they'd say *that's terrible, I'm so sorry you fell down the hole in the street, well done for getting out.* But it keeps on happening to you. Pretty soon, your friends are talking at parties, saying things like; *she's always falling down holes, she walks home alone, at night, on the bad roads, she's just really into unstable ground.* None of the holes I fell down were my boyfriends. One of them was someone else's boyfriend. If you were feeling cruel, you could say I brought it on myself. The hole's real girl-friend put on a white dress and married him, even though I told her everything. I try and warn people about the holes, I try and know where they are at various events, holes ordering pints at the poetry reading, holes as your friends' other friend, your lecturer, the hole, working on the role of the void in work by another hole. No one seems to listen. Sometimes they say *we're not all holes in the ground you know.* Or *you probably asked for it, you must love falling down holes. Why else would you stay? Didn't you tell the hole you loved it there even though you were scratching at the walls.* I don't know what to tell you except maybe the holes aren't part of the street. Maybe they're stacked on top of each other and when I hit rock bottom in this one, the next one is waiting to fall through.

Dust Bunny

The word tender

makes me ill

I don't like to think

of the texture of meat of bruises

shifting yellow when pressed

when I think of you now

I feel like a dust bunny or

the broken lipstick mirror

in the pocket of your rucksack

I give up professing love I'm trying

to turn the glitter cannon

on myself for once to hold

my anger that fistful of coins

in my teeth it's hard

it's hard every day

Foxes

I lie awake at night thinking of all the times I was told
to stay quiet. All the times I should have said nothing.

Listen, I am only a mangy fox among the recycling bins,
screeching to no one, chewing on my own tail. I know

I'm supposed to be checking over my shoulder
for something, but what? I keep expecting

the yellow window light of other people's houses
to bust open like a yolk and let me in. I keep waiting

to be picked up and held until I stop shaking
but I'm difficult to touch. Even the stars

are absenting themselves to the orange dark.
I sit at home, I lick my wounds. I chose

all of this, my job, this city, I pulled it close,
over and over with my grubby little hands.

Men's Rooms

are almost all the same. They're all built out of Lego bricks
or cardboard boxes. I've rifled through their books and learned
nothing, I've asked them about the meaning of their t shirts
and learned nothing. I've woken up again in nobody's corner,
a boxer on the back foot, waiting for something to happen.
But nothing ever does. Their curtains get progressively
less interesting, they have no knick knacks to pick up.
It's easy to do nothing there, it's easy to forget yourself.

I love you so much

I can feel it backing up like gunk in a drain. I am
just so clogged up with feeling. When I imagine you
sitting outside a cafe reading a book, I want my bones
to be scraped out and eaten. I want to be cooked down
into a rich sauce. I don't think I will ever have
any more good ideas, this was the last one.

Free Anna Delvey

a found poem

I need a nap
I've been up since I got out of prison
Prison is so exhausting you wouldn't know
I need a PR Person My DM's are out of control
I wish more people had my work ethic

lost interest in acquiring a boyfriend, looking for a job now
the only job I'm willing to accept at this stage of my career is
@GoldmanSachs creative director
Highbridge apartments for sale? I'm buying
Speak 4 languages in 6 voices
Come at me
Only I can mention me
Assessing the damage
I know what I'm doing
All your friends are mine now
Am an inch taller now from all that yoga I did in prison

Money is not an issue
I write better shit from a prison cell in a day than some of these
bitches with fifty editors do in a year
No one knows that Basic Instinct is really based on my life story
going to trial is the new sex tape
Can someone just tell me what to do already

I used to be thin

and dreadfully unhappy, every day I woke up and the happiness drained
out of me. I thought my unhappiness, my hunger, would go on forever
like the screaming darkness at the end of the sky, that nothing thrown into it
would ever reappear. I went to work, I smelled the steak, I soaked it in.
I thought of iron and blood, I chewed my fingertips. There was never enough
time for me to eat, nothing but six cups of coffee, nothing but
yorkshire puddings, we hid our glasses of water. I hallucinated, black cats
and grey rats, I told no one, because it didn't serve me. The heat was like
a boiled knife slipping through an ice cream cake. It was months
before I had enough to eat, I could have eaten every lobster
in the harbour and it wouldn't have filled me. My unhappiness
was like a steak knife, my hunger thrummed like a dishwasher in the dark.

Last night I dreamt I was alive and

put my foot through the surface of an ice pond put my foot
in a sock and ripped it put my foot in my mouth in front of
a crowd ate cardamom buns ate milk bottle sweets ate
oily fish from a can with a fork threw it up went out
to meet a friend hugged her hard and picked her up
picked myself up took myself out grabbed my own waist
through the velvet looked myself in the mirror
did finger guns felt something

Sex Scene

Your blood is my blood is your blood is my blood is your
blood is my blood is your blood is my blood is your blood
is my blood is your blood is my blood is your blood is my
blood is your blood is my blood is your blood is my blood is
your blood is my blood is your blood is my blood is your blood is mine.

the one girl gremlin

I posted the words *I am a gremlin trapped inside the body of a hot girl*
but also vice versa on the internet. The guy I had been out with twice
liked it. I wondered if he thought I was the hot girl or the gremlin.
I changed my display picture to a picture of the one girl gremlin.
She looked good, even better than I did. I don't expect to see the guy
I went out with twice ever again, except as part of some sort of terrible
accident. That whole month, the wind rattled the windows
of the shop I was working in, when I walked in the morning it ruined
my ponytail. I spent every spare minute looking at pictures of women's bodies
on the internet, trying to figure out what I looked like, trying to fit myself
into the snowstorm of images, I posted the words *is this site a mirror*
or a well and deleted them.

Cyberspace

I read somewhere that we do not enjoy the sound of women with high voices speaking. I read somewhere that we do not enjoy the sound of women with low voices speaking. I read somewhere I will never achieve universal acclaim. I read somewhere Diogenes lived in a wine vase and would emerge to criticise the people. I did a survey that said this would be the ideal career for me. I think everyone likes me better with long hair. I think I have exactly one healthy habit and it's eating dinner at 6.30pm. I was right to spend all those years afraid to be in public. I read somewhere it would be better if I didn't do anything at all. I read somewhere the gap is widening. I read somewhere that rioting is effective. I read somewhere the super rich will flee to Mars and the rest of us will do what we need to do. I don't get ready, I stay ready. I read somewhere I am not to be trusted. Some people were harmed in the making of these poems. I read that desire will continue and it will be embarrassing. I'm not going to get it right this time, no matter how much I want to.

Dolly Parton enters a Dolly Parton lookalike contest in a gay bar and does not place

After Chrissy Williams

Some days I can't get up to be myself, it is too painful and boring to climb into the suit. In the Winter I get so blue it's like getting fired, every day, from the musical based on your life. Sometimes there is a Phoebe Stuckes lookalike contest and I'm not even allowed in the village hall. Not even Dolly Parton could get on the shortlist to be Dolly Parton, Kylie Minogue competed to be Kylie and came third. I couldn't be Dolly on any day of the year, least of all Christmas, where she sings in all white, surrounded by all five of her sisters. I want to be Barbara Windsor, on her Barbara Windsor float, looking like a miniature Barbara Windsor, partying with the Barbara Windsors twice her size.

Baby you know what I want

to howl at the moon crawl into a lake on my stomach and never come out
come out 1000 years later and drink blood from a live animal seduce a man
just by standing there seduce a woman by loving her unconditionally
stop feeling guilty for killing everything green I touch stop feeling guilty
for never embodying Joan of Arc or any other androgynous saint portrayed
in a stained glass window stand under a disco ball for Thelma Houston's
Don't Leave Me This Way to be playing blue eyeshadow feather boa
lip gloss thermal rollers false eyelashes to give it up give it up give it up

Jane Fonda

I'm with Jane Fonda on this one, I never wanted a husband until I got stuck in my evening dress, it was like being digested by a velvet anaconda. When I got sober in the morning I burst forth like a cuttlefish out of its shell. I hope Jane Fonda was doing something similar, hobbling around her kitchen in her dressing gown, her feet aching from the night before. Maybe she has people for that, to bring her coffee, perhaps she holds out a hand and it's there. I hope so. She supports a number of important causes, when she got arrested at a climate change protest her coat was white, it matched the zip ties on her wrists, how impossibly chic. I like to see her and Lily Tomlin together, causing trouble, talking over each other. I have a postcard that says LILY TOMLIN FOR PRESIDENT and I think Jane Fonda would agree, we love you Jane Fonda.

Crows

when my anger dissipated
not even birds
were afraid of me
Geese accepted me
as one their own,
I sat on the grass
their young gathered
around me
pigeons made
loving sounds
at my feet.
Crows grabbed
at my friend's head
pecked it, drew blood
I walked back
the same way
they were unfazed,
quiet black shoes
on the wire.
Horses rested
when I was near.
Foxes walked
in my slip stream
They knew
I had been bristling
for four years,
and in this year,
the quiet year
I had gone
soft.

Pastoral

At home I have this urge to walk into the woods,
barefoot in a white chemise. I plait my hair and
think about the girl in the rural horror film, her face
crumpling like the bumper on a totalled car.

I want to be like her, pour my heart out to strangers,
wear flowers, hold hands. When you give me
the silent treatment I imagine you as a deer,
resting your thorny head in my lap. Lately

in my nightmares, you're turning your face away
while I reverse a pickup truck into a lake.
My room is full of money spiders, I stay up late

killing them, they go for my eyes. I think I could have joined
Heaven's Gate. They were all looking for something.
I grow my hair long, I want to be lifted up.

Killbuck

I have dreams about this woman and her post on the advice forum. A calf died on her doorstep, for no reason. Her back pain prevented her from moving it herself. Her husband said he would *take care of it*. Her husband cancelled the removal company's appointment. The husband cut the calf into pieces, strew the pieces over their land. Other animals came to feast on it. The neighbouring farms complained. The coyotes moved closer from the hills.

Poem in which I am always leaving

You love him but not in a good way. Your family are gravely concerned. You watch the fungus gnats climbing the window, you are killing your plants with attention. Your mother is sending you a stack of jumpers. Your mother thinks walking away was the right thing to do. You miss things from your old life, the sensation of counting money, the imprint of someone else's tongue on your own. You think if someone were to tuck a strand of hair behind your ear you would die from it. You think you would flinch. You used to flinch whenever someone reached their hand out towards you, but it was for other reasons. Sometimes you cannot remember what those reasons were. Sometimes you remember all the reasons at once. You experience anger only in retrograde. You wonder why you ever thought everything was fine. You think the waves of anger are better than the fear. The fear was all consuming. You could not sit calmly, even with a man who loved you. Eventually you fled from the room.

It's a bad business

-poetry. Often I would rather be buying a croissant,
doing something to improve my quality of life.
Last year I did my own taxes and it was almost as bad
as poetry. Looks like I'll be doing my taxes for the rest of my life,
and why? Because of poetry. It's sexy but inconsistent. You're just like that-
poetry. The last time you broke up with me it was like getting whacked
with a stick at a party thrown by my dearest friend and you know what
came out of the piñata? Poetry. I guess it's just my silly life, my insides
that have to be knitted into poetry. I do the one thing I was sent here to do,
I set fire to a number of disappointing fireworks sequentially- poetry.

ACKNOWLEDGEMENTS:

'Paris' previously appeared in *The Poetry Review*. I would like to thank the following people: Jack Wrighton, Catriona Bolt and Emily Meller for reading early drafts, offering their thoughts and encouragement and Stuart Bartholomew for all his help in putting this pamphlet together including making it look nice. Additionally, I would like to thank my mother Jane for always enjoying my writing and also for keeping me in mint aero during the first lockdown even though she is a vegan.

ABOUT THE AUTHOR:

Phoebe Stuckes is a writer from West Somerset now living in London. She has been a winner of the Foyle Young Poets award four times and is a former Barbican Young Poet. Her writing has appeared in *Poetry Review, The Rialto, The North* and *Ambit* among others. Her debut pamphlet, *Gin & Tonic* was shortlisted for The Michael Marks Award 2017. She has been awarded an Eric Gregory Award and The Geoffrey Dearmer Prize. Her first full length collection, *Platinum Blonde* was published by Bloodaxe Books in 2020.

ABOUT VERVE POETRY PRESS

Verve Poetry Press is a quite new and already award-winning press that focussed initially on meeting a local need in Birmingham - a need for the vibrant poetry scene here in Brum to find a way to present itself to the poetry world via publication. Co-founded by Stuart Bartholomew and Amerah Saleh, it now publishes poets from all corners of the UK and beyond - poets that speak to the city's varied and energetic qualities and will contribute to its many poetic stories.

Added to this is a colourful pamphlet series, many featuring poets who have performed at our sister festival - and a poetry show series which captures the magic of longer poetry performance pieces by festival alumni such as Polarbear, Matt Abbott and Genevieve Carver.

The press has been voted Most Innovative Publisher at the Saboteur Awards, and has won the Publisher's Award for Poetry Pamphlets at the Michael Marks Awards.

Like the festival, we strive to think about poetry in inclusive ways and embrace the multiplicity of approaches towards this glorious art.

www.vervepoetrypress.com
@VervePoetryPres
mail@vervepoetrypress.com